I want to be confident

For everyone who ever told me:
Yes, you can!

Other books in the *I want to...* series:

I want to sleep
I want to be calm
I want to be organised
I want to be happy

I want to be confident

LIVING, WORKING AND COMMUNICATING WITH CONFIDENCE

———————— BY ————————

Harriet Griffey

hardie grant books

Contents

Introduction: What is confidence? 7
Quiz: How confident are you? 13
Who am I? 17
Self-worth, self-esteem, self-assurance 23
Barriers to confidence 29
Authenticity & confidence style 35
What's stopping you? 39
Basic confidence skills 45
Physical confidence 49
Body language & other communication 57
Thinking confidently about yourself 63
Practising confidence 69
Acting confidently – or 'fake it 'til you make it' 73
First impressions – why they count 79
Addressing anxiety, taking risks & embracing the unknown 87

Social confidence & dealing with nerves **95**
Importance of listening **101**
Dating **107**
Work & business confidence **113**
Job interviews **119**
Presentation skills & public speaking **125**
Conclusion: Confident you! **133**
Acknowledgements **138**
Appendix **139**
About the author **141**
Index **142**

What is confidence?

Confidence is feeling emotionally sure, secure and strong; it's the opposite of feeling fearful, anxious or scared. It's knowing in your heart that you are safe, capable and talented; and can accomplish – or at least, try to accomplish – whatever it is you want to do.

It's not the mountain we conquer but ourselves. *Edmund Hillary*

Some people just seem more confident than others, especially from the outside; but bear in mind that even the most confident person you meet will have had times when they lacked, or have had a crisis of, confidence. It's all part of human nature to feel unsure about new situations and events, but it's through the experience of these that we learn how to do things and gain confidence from doing them.

Self-confidence is also about having an internalised belief in oneself, built on one's past successful experiences. And it's how we learn to become confident. As a child, for example, the first time you tried to pour water into a cup may have been difficult, frustrating and even upsetting, especially if you spilled it. But with a bit of patient help and practice, it became easier. Soon you were confident of your ability to do it; and also confident about being able to mop it up if you did spill it. Success! And from small beginnings like these, big steps in confidence were made.

Don't wait until everything is just right. It will never be perfect. There will always be challenges, obstacles and less-than-perfect conditions. So what. Get started now. With each step you take, you will grow stronger and stronger, more and more skilled, more and more self-confident and more and more successful. *Mark Victor Hansen*

Samuel Beckett's suggestion that we should not be put off when we fail, but that we try again and *fail better*, suggests that instead of dismissing ourselves as failures, we should look at what failed and try again – not harder, but *differently*. When we try differently, we learn from what didn't work last time and try a new approach. But we should not be put off when things don't work out the first time, because it's through these learning processes that we build our confidence, whether it is learning to ride a bike, giving a presentation, or going on a first date. With repetition, practice and preparation it gets easier and, importantly, we gain further confidence by continuing in our efforts, seeing the effort itself as worthwhile. Failing is not the problem and our efforts don't always fail. However, not trying at all *is* a problem as this rules out the possibility of any success.

Ever tried. Ever failed. No matter. Try again. Fail again. Fail better.

SAMUEL BECKETT

Low self-confidence isn't a life sentence. Self-confidence can be learned, practised and mastered – just like any other skill. Once you master it, everything in your life will change for the better.

BARRIE DAVENPORT

How confident are you?

> **When you're out and about, do you generally find other people:**
A Very friendly.
B Approachable.
C OK – I don't really notice.
D Generally unhelpful and sometimes difficult.

> **At a workplace social event, do you immediately:**
A Breeze up to the nearest person and start talking.
B Take a deep breath and look for someone you know.
C Take a quick look and if there's no one you know, leave.
D Never go to these events unless it's with a friend.

> **Do you feel that your opinion matters?**
A Yes.
B Yes, but not everyone will agree with me.
C No, no one's interested.
D Don't have an opinion.

> **If you try something new and it doesn't work, do you think:**
A It was fine.
B I'll have another go, but maybe try differently.
C That always happens to me, I'm useless.
D I won't try that again.

> **When you've completed a task successfully, do you think:**
A I knew I could do it.
B I wasn't sure, but I thought I probably could.
C That was easier than I thought.
D That was a fluke, maybe I got it wrong.

> **Given a complex problem to solve, do you:**
A Tackle it alone, pretty sure you can work it out.
B Take a look and then ask for help.
C Take a look and then give up.
D Don't bother to try, it's too difficult.

> **If you make a mistake, do you feel:**
A Fine, it's just a mistake.
B OK, but maybe I'll try again differently.
C Terrible – such an idiot!
D Furious with yourself and can't let it go.

> **Do you find it hard to say no?**
A Never.
B Occasionally.
C Often.
D Always.

> **How successful do you think you are compared to your peer group?**
A Generally, I'm more successful.
B I don't know, I don't really make comparisons.
C Everyone is more successful than me.
D I'm a complete failure by comparison.

> **How much do you care what people think of you?**
A I don't care at all.
B Generally, I only care about what those I care about think of me.
C Some days it matters more than others.
D I judge everything by what others think of me.

> **If your spouse/partner/lover does something that upsets you, can you tell them how you feel?**
A Always.
B Often.
C Occasionally.
D Never.

> **The night before an important exam/test/interview, how well do you sleep?**
A Fine.
B Fine – have prepared well and am not worried.
C Awake early, worrying.
D Awake several times in the night, worrying.

Score your answers

A = 4 points
B = 3 points
C = 2 points
D = 1 point

Score between 48 and 36 points
You are generally pretty self-confident and
also willing to learn from experience, which also
helps build confidence. Sometimes, though,
if your confidence is too extreme, it could be worth
toning down how you express it a little, so you don't
intimidate others less confident than yourself – use
your confidence to encourage theirs!

Score between 35 and 24 points
Some days, if events aren't too challenging, your confidence is OK.
On other days, you probably need to practise your skills or 'fake it'
a little. You can also learn from the positive experiences you have
and remind yourself about past successes to help you become more
confident that things will work out well.

Score between 23 and 12 points
Confidence can be something of a struggle and you may need
to question some of your self-beliefs about what you can't do,
boosting your confidence by reminding yourself what you can do,
and building on that. Take regular opportunities to challenge your
negative ideas and push yourself a little to increase your confidence
more regularly, stepping outside your comfort zone gradually.

Who am I?

'Who am I?' is a question asked by philosophers and thinkers, as well as ourselves, as we work out who and what we are, and how we want to live our lives, trying on lots of ideas for size along the way. By a process of trial and error, and a constantly changing landscape of experience, we can arrive at a place where we are confident about the person we are. This is very much a learnt process, influenced by what we choose to make of our life experiences and choices.

Do you consider yourself a confident person? Or, perhaps, do you feel confident on some occasions but not others? While you may have a job where you feel comfortable, do social occasions make you nervous? Whatever your experience, it's reassuring to know that at any stage of life you can learn to be more confident. What can be helpful, though, is to understand where any personal lack of confidence might be rooted.

Does being an introvert make a difference?

Many introverts are confident people and introversion is not about lack of confidence, but characterises those who are more stimulated by internal thought than by external action and interaction. Where an introverted personality type might not actively seek and enjoy large social interactions, this is a preference rather than an aversion. They just prefer the solace of solitude, at least at regular intervals, to recharge their batteries. To a more extroverted person, this may seem like shyness or a resistance to participation. If you are an introvert, you and others may mistake this preference for lack of confidence. You may also feel socially inadequate in some way because of it. By recognising and understanding this aspect of your personality, you can work with it rather than be floored by it, learning ways to manage other people's expectations as well as your own.

Bill Gates, founder of Microsoft and one of the most successful businessmen in the world, is, by nature, an introvert, but he definitely doesn't lack self-confidence. By contrast, Barbra Streisand is a hugely successful, award-winning singer, actress and film producer, with a larger-than-life extrovert personality. She has, at times, suffered from crippling stage fright. Both have learnt how their personalities affect them and have worked with, rather than against, this to become successful, confident people.

Can extroverts lack confidence?

Yes. Although extroverts are stimulated by action and interaction outside their own thoughts, they might still lack confidence in certain situations. We are all a mixture of circumstance and experience, along with any genetic predisposition. Like everyone else, extroverts learn what they feel confident about through experience. The difference is that they may be more willing to try new experiences, take risks and generally open themselves up to learning, and feeling more confident about these experiences.

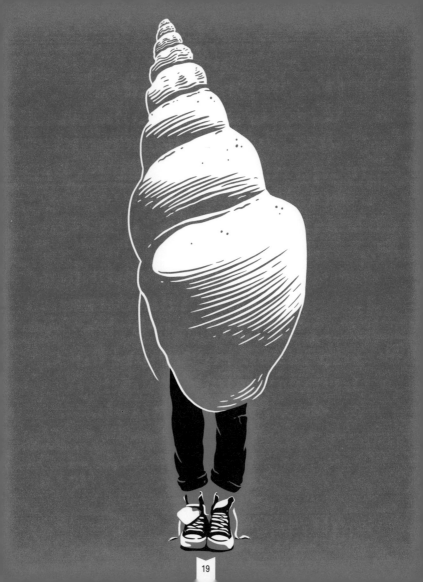

We often marvel at how introverted, geeky kids 'blossom' into secure and happy adults. We liken it to a metamorphosis. However, maybe it's not the children who change but their environments. As adults they get to select the careers, spouses and social circles that suit them. They don't have to live in whatever culture they're plonked into.

SUSAN CAIN, AUTHOR OF *QUIET: THE POWER OF INTROVERT*

What about shyness?

Shyness isn't the same as introversion. In many ways, shyness is a learnt experience and is characterised by self-consciousness, negative self-evaluation and self-preoccupation. Some people may be more prone towards shyness, and this may be more true of introverts but not exclusively so. Some people may be more shy at particular times of their lives. Adolescence, for example, is often characterised by extreme self-consciousness and preoccupation that creates shyness. So much so that these are accepted facets of adolescent experience, but ones that most people 'grow out of' as they mature. However, for some, shyness can become crippling, linked to extreme anxiety and can make life miserable. The good news about shyness, however, is that there are many things that can help in learning to manage it, from cognitive behavioural therapy (CBT, see page 30) to utilising some of the social tools that help create a confident attitude and, in time, greater confidence itself.

I have made plenty of mistakes. The key to life is to learn from them. I have been a little too introspective, but I think that stemmed from insecurity or shyness. I took a long time to grow up. *Richard Gere, actor and Buddhist*

Self-worth, self-esteem, self-assurance

What do these have to do with becoming more confident? The clue is in the prefix, self. But let's break it down and see what might be useful to consider in the pursuit of self-confidence.

Self-worth

Sometimes used to mean the same as self-esteem, this is more about the sense of your own worth as a person, and the value you give to yourself. While it's useful to acknowledge and take pleasure in our achievements, the downside of this is that continually comparing ourselves to others and their achievements can be unhelpful, as there will always be those who apparently do better or worse than us.

Comparison is the thief of joy.

THEODORE ROOSEVELT

Self-assurance

Assurance is about certainty and freedom from doubt; self-assurance comes from having confidence not just in your own abilities but also in yourself. The assurance comes from that belief. We experience this when someone assures us of something and it happens. Self-assurance is the same – believing it and having that self-belief – and this all contributes to our self-confidence.

Because one believes in oneself, one doesn't try to convince others. Because one is content with oneself, one doesn't need others' approval. Because one accepts oneself, the whole world accepts him or her. *Lao-Tzu*

Self-esteem

What is your opinion of yourself? Do you have high self-esteem? While we generally value high self-esteem, it can sometimes come from a place of comparison rather than an authentic, secure sense of self, and its downside can sometimes be a sort of defensive narcissism. When this happens, confidence comes from elevating your position above that of your peers, rather than from a self-assured place where comparison is irrelevant. Boosting your own ego at the expense of others is not beneficial, because when we fail, we are bereft. Self-esteem has to come from a more secure place than narcissism.

If your self-esteem is too closely linked to what other people think of you, this can be unhelpful because it's actually quite difficult to really know what they might be thinking and you could end up making assumptions that are wrong. And why should it matter to you what someone – whom you don't know very well and who doesn't know you very well – thinks of you, anyway? It pays to use a little perspective here.

It took me a long time not to judge myself through someone else's eyes.

SALLY FIELD

Self-compassion

A better place to start from, argues Kristin Neff, psychology professor and author of a book on the subject, is self-compassion. This way, you treat yourself as your own best friend would when you screw up, encouraging yourself, telling yourself that it wasn't so bad and to give it another go.

I found in my research that the biggest reason people aren't more self-compassionate is that they are afraid they'll become self-indulgent. They believe self-criticism is what keeps them in line. Most people have gotten it wrong because our culture says being hard on yourself is the way to be. **KRISTIN NEFF**

Barriers to confidence

If you feel that lack of confidence is an issue for you, it can sometimes be that you have used strategies in the past that have become barriers to what you want to achieve now. For example, you may have avoided doing things about which you had no confidence, and that was one strategy. You may be unconfident about public speaking, for example, so you've just not done it. That strategy has worked but it's kept you stuck and become a barrier that would be useful to address. Identifying personal barriers to confidence can be the first step in overcoming them.

We either make ourselves happy or miserable. The amount of work is the same. *Carlos Castaneda*

Address the issue

Once you know what's inhibiting your confidence, you can take steps to overcome this. For example, if you find talking to people you don't know difficult, practise saying hello to the person who serves you in a shop rather than just handing over the money silently, and build from there. If there's a job you'd like to apply for, but don't know whether you have the necessary skills, find out more about it. Ask for help. Show initiative. Through such small initial steps can big changes be made.

> **You can't always control what goes on outside. But you can always control what goes on inside.** *Wayne Dyer*

Negative thoughts

That voice in your head? The one that says you can't, or you're not good enough, or you'll fail? Remember that you're in charge here. You can use that voice to say, 'I can do it! I'm great. And, well, if it doesn't succeed first time, I'll find a way.' By changing the voice (thoughts) in your head, you can change what you believe about yourself, which is the basis of CBT (see page 21). Because if you can't be on your own side, how are you going to convince anyone else? Give it a go. Every time that inner critic (see page 39) shows up, change the way you respond, rewrite the script, say something positive rather than negative: 'I can', rather than 'I can't'.

Do not allow negative thoughts to enter your mind for they are the weeds that strangle confidence.

BRUCE LEE

Believe you can and you're halfway there.

THEODORE ROOSEVELT

Build confidence

What are you good at? Lots of things, probably, that you take for granted, but for the purpose of this exercise, focus on one small thing and build on it. Get better at it. Extend its possibilities. Turn an interest into a passion and a conviction. Become that expert. Share your skills. In addition, if there's something you're not great at but would like to improve, give it a go. If you want to run a marathon, the first thing you have to do is get off the couch. This applies to *everything*, including building and improving on your confidence.

Authenticity & confidence style

Be faithful to that which exists within yourself. *André Gide*

Be yourself

This may seem obvious but it's essential if you want to have authentic self-confidence. Take steps to show up as the best version of yourself: do what's necessary to enhance your confidence and find a style that feels comfortable to you. There's no point concerning yourself with trying to control what other people think, as you can't ever know for sure. Plus, if you were to ask 20 different people what they think, you'd probably get 20 different opinions. Remember, too, that those around you can only see what you choose to show them: they are on the outside looking at a complete package – *you*. You might feel nervous on the inside – and that's the time to use some of those confidence tools (see pages 87–92) to reinforce your confidence and show them the best of yourself.

Be who you are and say what you feel, because those who mind don't matter, and those who matter don't mind.
Bernard M. Baruch

Being comfortable with and accepting who we are comes from knowing and trusting ourselves. For many of us this can feel like a lifelong journey as we react to and interact with those around us. At our core, our personality remains fairly constant and this is something we can always draw on.

If you're by nature an introvert, for example, you can make your quieter, observational style work for you. If you are more extrovert in personality, your natural inclination towards sociability may help. Comparing yourself with others isn't necessarily helpful, but it can be useful to see how other people manage situations and what might, or might not, work for you.

I've finally stopped running away from myself. Who else is there better to be? *Goldie Hawn*

Always be yourself, express yourself and have faith in yourself. Do not go out and look for a successful personality and duplicate it.

BRUCE LEE

What's stopping you?

Now, take a moment to consider what might be getting in the way of your confidence: what is it that might be stopping you becoming a more confident person? A bit of reflection can help you work this out.

It's never too late to be what you might have been. *George Eliot*

Inner critic

Often what stops you can be as simple as that internal, self-critical voice, the one in your head that constantly

There came a time when the risk to remain tight in the bud was more painful than the risk it took to blossom.

ANAÏS NIN

judges and snipes at you, undermining your confidence. This voice is seldom rooted in reality – how do you know, *really*, what that stranger in the train carriage thinks of you?

Challenge it. That critical voice is sapping your confidence. Question it. What actual evidence do you have for what it's telling you? In reality, you can have no real idea of what another person thinks, and the look on their face probably has nothing to do with you but comes from their own thoughts, anxieties and preoccupations. Why should you care, anyway? Counter your inner critic with more positive affirmations – those that are as accepting, tolerant and loving of yourself as you would like to be of those around you.

No one can make you feel inferior without your consent.
Eleanor Roosevelt

Self-sabotage

This can be a feature of our inner critic. Sometimes, when we are unconfident about something, we unconsciously do things that either stop us trying, or prove ourselves right. We set ourselves up to fail, and then tell ourselves, *'There, I was right, I knew it was impossible.'* Self-sabotage is an unhelpful strategy because, ultimately, it prevents you from doing things that could be successful and might help enhance your confidence about future efforts.

Imposter syndrome

This is akin to self-sabotage, but very different from faking it (see page 73) because it stems from a lack of self-belief. You imagine that you will be somehow found out as an imposter, not really capable of what you say you can do – even though you're doing it! This comes from an insecure place within and sometimes happens when we've made a recent step in progress but our confidence in our ability to do so has not kept pace. Instead of thinking what's been achieved is good, it's undermined by the suspicion that we'll somehow get found out. This is also a voice that the inner critic sometimes uses: identify it for what it is, then ignore it.

Catastrophising

Imagining the worst might feel like making good preparation for an unforeseen event, but there's a difference between doing a reasonable risk assessment – *It looks like rain, I'll take an umbrella* – and assuming that something cataclysmic could happen. This just creates unnecessary anxiety, which, in turn, saps confidence.

Imagining a catastrophe around every corner can sometimes come from a place of somewhat bizarre logic or magical thinking where, at a subconscious level, we convince ourselves that by imagining the worst, the imagining of it somehow stops the worst from happening. We even have evidence to prove that imagining the worst works: we thought it might happen, it didn't happen, so therefore our thinking of it must have *stopped* it happening. None of which, rationally, is true. The worst didn't happen because it seldom does; worrying about something that probably won't happen is just unhelpful and undermines confidence. Learning from past experience and changing your thinking on this will remove a huge amount of anxiety and you will automatically feel more confident.

Overthinking

It's one thing to be prepared but it can be unhelpful to overthink a situation, to focus on worst-case scenarios to the point where the idea of what could (but probably won't) happen makes you so anxious, you won't even try. There's no point undermining your own confidence by persistently focusing on what can go wrong. Better, instead, to ensure you have done what you can, then let it go. Remember the times when the worst didn't happen? That's a far more accurate view of life, so focus on that.

Basic confidence skills

We all know what a confident person looks like, right? We all know someone about whom we've probably thought: *they* know how to do it, *they* always look relaxed and confident. We see people who inspire confidence in us. What is it about them? Can we break it down, identify it – and then use some of those skills ourselves?

As former US president Barack Obama famously said, 'Yes we can.'

What does a confident person look like?

This has nothing to do with what they're actually wearing, although they are probably dressed appropriately for the situation they're in, their clothes fit well, are clean and pressed, without tears or buttons missing. They look like someone who takes personal pride in how they present themselves. They may show a sense of personal style, but this is in keeping and adds to their confidence, without detracting or distracting from it.

They may even look like Obama. He had the most difficult job in the world, but he looked confident doing it.

What do they do?

Do you notice the way they stand? Talk? Listen? You'll probably notice that they stand or sit still, in a relaxed way without fidgeting. Do they greet you with good eye contact and a smile, and do they extend their hand? You will probably notice how a confident person will look you in the eye, holding your gaze, nodding occasionally while you talk, maybe smiling. Their body language and gestures are open and friendly. They seem sure of who they are and what they're doing.

In addition, confident people tend to listen well, ask questions and respond positively to other people's ideas and suggestions. They are assertive but polite, and don't take things too personally or themselves too seriously.

What can we do?

Having observed a confident person in action, and bearing in mind the above, you can see that there are skills being used. These skills may have come naturally to that person or they may have been learnt. It doesn't really matter. The point is that they are being used – and *you* can learn and use these skills, too. You can make a choice about how you want to show up in any situation and you can harness the skills necessary to do so confidently.

Because of the self-confidence with which he had spoken, no one could tell whether what he said was very clever or very stupid. *Leo Tolstoy*

Remember... we see those around us from the outside in; we see ourselves from the inside out. People who look relaxed and confident may not feel quite the same inside but they are projecting confidence – and that's what you see and respond to. You can do the same and be seen in this way, too.

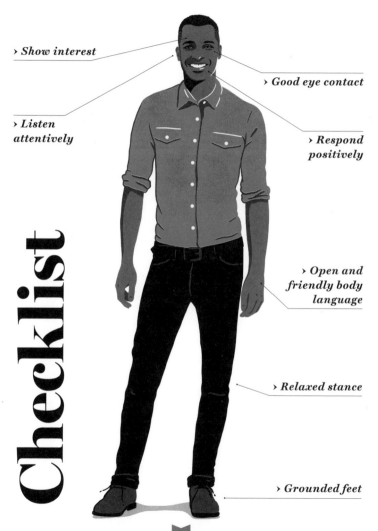

› Show interest

› Good eye contact

› Listen attentively

› Respond positively

› Open and friendly body language

› Relaxed stance

› Grounded feet

Checklist

Physical confidence

Pause for a moment and remember what it's like to feel unconfident, nervous and unsure. Remind yourself of what your body felt like and how you felt, *physically*, at that point: shaky and tense, perhaps? Now you're going to think about how you can improve your *physical* confidence and how that can, in turn, improve your feelings of confidence overall.

Get connected

We spend so long sitting and many of us work solely in our heads. This means that we can become very disconnected from our physical selves and our bodies become somehow alien to us. Floppy muscle tone makes us feel unsupported, literally, and we can feel as if we are dragging ourselves through life rather than moving with energetic action and confident ease. Poor muscle tone also creates an over-reliance on ligaments and tendons to keep us functioning, running the risk of tendonitis, back ache and repetitive strain injury. Our posture, digestion and circulation is compromised, too, making our bodies complain rather than carry us with strength, grace and confidence.

Exercise because you love your body, not because you hate it.

ANON

Get physical

Your body was built for movement. All the time we spend sitting at a desk leads to sloppy posture, poor abdominals, weak legs and slumped shoulders; and if we never exercise, then this is what we're left with when we stand up. Not an impressive, inspiring or confident picture, is it? This is then communicated to others through our body language (see page 57).

Regular exercise will improve muscle tone, core strength and posture; will relieve aches and pains; and, whatever your build, it will immediately improve the way you look, as you stand up straighter, tummy tucked in and shoulders relaxed but squared. Factor regular exercise into your life so it becomes routine – a walk to work, a weekly yoga or Pilates class, swimming, football, tennis – and you will soon notice that by feeling better about yourself physically, how you stand and move will improve and you'll automatically feel more physically confident.

The importance of breath

A poor physique and posture inhibits breathing, restricting it to the upper chest. This means we tend to breathe poorly, in the way that we do when we are nervous, but *all the time*. It works both ways: breathing in the way that you do when you're nervous has the effect of telling your body you are! Conversely, if you breathe in the way that you would if you were relaxed, confident, assured – this conveys to your body that you are (even if you're not!), reinforcing a sense of control over your body's reactions.

This makes your breath one of your best tools for calming and focusing your mind, which will make you feel more confident. So, learning to breathe well, which goes hand in hand with good posture, is an important part of improving self-confidence. Regular practice will make this automatically available to you when you need it.

AND BREATHE...

- Lie comfortably on the floor, knees bent, chin tucked in; or sit upright in a chair, legs uncrossed, feet flat and grounded on the floor.
- Consciously relax your neck and shoulders, rest your arms by your sides with your palms turned upwards.
- Breathe long and gently through your nose, into your belly until you see it gently rise, for a slow count of five.
- Pause, and hold that breath for a count of five, then gently exhale through your mouth for another slow count of five.
- While doing this, try to clear your mind of all other thoughts or, if this is difficult, close your eyes and visualise a pebble dropping into a pool of water and gently sinking, slowly, down.
- Repeat this breathing cycle 10 times, then see how your regular breathing adjusts.
- You can also use this breathing technique at any time you feel tense or stressed, or as the basis of any meditation practice.

If you want to conquer the anxiety of life, live in the moment, live in the breath.

AMIT RAY

Be body confident

One of the benefits of being physically confident is that it can give you a sense of being grounded and secure, which can be enhanced by regular exercise. Yoga, in particular, is a practice that aligns the body with the breath, activates the body's energy via the feet, which are grounded, while the core is strong and the shoulders relaxed. Yoga postures create both body awareness and strength, and postures like Warrior Pose can make you feel both physically and emotionally strong. T'ai chi works, too, in a similarly effective way.

Stay grounded

Feel the contact with the ground (or floor) and be aware of how solid, stable, secure and reliable it feels. Connect with that and this will, in turn, make you feel more secure, stable and confident, up through your body. Make sure that your weight is evenly spread through your feet (practise this barefoot) from the heel to the ball of your foot and through all the toes, and that your knees aren't locked but gently supportive.

Posture

Your posture will be improved by your body confidence and posture is often the first thing someone else will notice about you. Good posture makes you look poised, alert and engaged. It's part of your body language (see page 57) and can immediately convey confidence if you are standing or sitting up straight, with relaxed shoulders, arms and hands, and with your chin tucked, looking your companion or colleague in the eye.

It's critical to know that changing the way you carry your body will change the way you feel about yourself. So sit up straight, not to respect others, but yourself. It will make you more affecting. *Amy Cuddy, social psychologist*

Body language & other communication

Very powerful messages can be communicated non-verbally via body language, so it's worth understanding what it is, how it works and how you can use it to your advantage, both to enhance and convey a sense of personal confidence. Professor Albert Mehrabian, psychologist and author of *Silent Messages*, has suggested that when it comes to communicating attitudes and feelings, this is expressed 7 per cent by what is said, 38 per cent by the tone of voice and 55 per cent by body language.

Facial expression

A relaxed, alert and focused facial expression, with good eye contact, conveys warmth and interest and indicates that you are engaged and paying attention to what is being said. Occasionally smiling and nodding, where appropriate and without interrupting verbally, can also be encouraging to others, and promotes good two-way communication.

Eye rolling is one of the nonverbal signs that is pretty much always aggressive.

STEVE WATTS

Tone of voice

Speaking confidently means being heard, but the tone of voice you use also speaks volumes. You can inject warmth into your tone by smiling as you speak, which also helps reduce any tension in your voice that could make you sound a little aggressive. Pausing to breathe adequately when you speak will also help you relax, modulate your voice and sound more confident. Volume, too, is important: being able to lower the pitch of your voice while raising it in volume will work better than shouting. Avoid making a statement a question by raising your pitch at the end of a sentence. Known technically as a 'high rising terminal' or upspeak, the implied questioning can make you sound unsure and deferential.

Posture

While an upright, relaxed posture promotes confidence, in yourself and others, a closed posture, designed to protect and hide the body, where the shoulders are hunched and the arms and legs crossed, suggests anxiety and hostility. Deliberately using an open posture will also help you feel more relaxed. Use relaxation techniques (see page 91) to help, and this will make you feel more confident.

I speak two languages. Body and English. *Mae West*

Touching

This is another way of communicating with others non-verbally. The amount or type of touching can vary from a gentle touch on the upper arm, to a handshake, a hug or a kiss. The form it takes is highly dependent on the relationship between those communicating and the context. The levels of socially acceptable touching also vary in different cultures, so it's important to pay attention and match your level of touching with what's appropriate. Generally, the more formal the relationship or situation, the less touching occurs. If in doubt, or if you think it will make someone uncomfortable, don't touch; or restrict touch to the upper arm or to shaking hands.

USE NON-VERBAL COMMUNICATION TO SOFTEN
Smile / **O**pen posture / **F**orward lean / **T**ouch / **E**ye contact / **N**od

---

Gestures

Closely allied to touching are the gestures you make when you communicate. Fidgeting, cracking your knuckles, picking your cuticles all convey nervousness and are distracting to those around you, even if you are unaware of what you're doing. By contrast, when you use your hands spontaneously to make open, expansive gestures as you speak, to support or emphasise what you are saying, these can be encouraging and inclusive.

The human body is the best picture of the human soul.

LUDWIG WITTGENSTEIN

Personal space

We all feel more comfortable, relaxed and confident if our personal space is respected and this is very much dependent on the situation we're in – whether this is intimate, social or formal. It's worth considering how you work within your personal space and that of others, when you want to appear confident within a specific relationship.

INTIMATE DISTANCE for embracing, touching or whispering

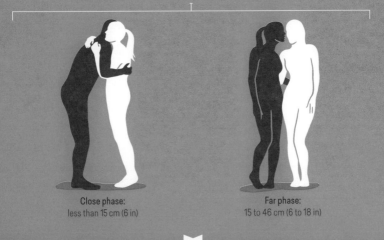

Close phase:
less than 15 cm (6 in)

Far phase:
15 to 46 cm (6 to 18 in)

PERSONAL DISTANCE for interactions among good friends or family members

Close phase:
46 to 76 cm (1 ft 6 in to 2 ft 6 in)

Far phase:
76 to 122 cm (2ft 6 in to 4 ft)

SOCIAL DISTANCE for interactions among acquaintances

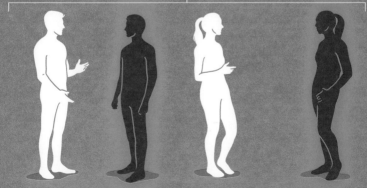

Close phase:
1.2 to 2.1 m (4 to 7 ft)

Far phase:
2.1 to 3.7 m (7 to 12 ft)

Thinking confidently about yourself

When it comes to thinking confidently about yourself, you are your own best resource. Always focus on and remember what's positive, instead of what's negative, and on what you *can* do as opposed to what you can't. Be your own best friend.

Your inner voice

This is where that voice in your head needs to be one of your very best friends – a friend who is 100 per cent on your side, telling you that the glass is half full rather than half empty and that you *can* do it. This may appear to be a cliché but it is rooted in truth. Your thoughts are your own, so the best choice you can make is to think confidently about yourself.

A man is but the product of his thoughts: what he thinks, he becomes.

GANDHI

Talk to yourself like you would to someone you love.

BRENÉ BROWN

TOP TIPS
- Remember that occasion when something went really well for you? Focus on what worked and use it.
- If you feel fearful, remember that this is probably because you're about to do something that, in the long run, will make you more, not less, confident.
- Don't make assumptions about other people and how they see you: work on the basis of fact – what you know rather than what you don't.
- Don't overcomplicate whatever it is you have to do: break it down into manageable chunks.
- Don't waste time on things that didn't work out: review them, take what's useful and move on.
- Promote positivity, even when you don't feel it, as it will attract positivity from others.

That's not to say that there won't be days when the challenge to think confidently is greater than on others. Days when you have to muster courage and conviction to step up to the mark and deliver the best version of yourself. So be proactive. Make a conscious choice to see the positive, because it makes better sense to choose what serves you (the positive) rather than what doesn't (the negative).

Trust yourself. Create the kind of self that you will be happy to live with all your life. Make the most of yourself by fanning the tiny, inner sparks of possibility into flames of achievement. *Golda Meir*

Practising confidence

How confident you feel day by day can fluctuate, depending on your state of mind and what you have to do. There will always be some days when you feel more confident than others. On those days, when it's more of a struggle, bear in mind those things you *can* do to restore your confidence. Recognise this fluctuation for what it is. Don't beat yourself up about it, but do remember that you can practise confidence, and then resort to what you know works best when your confidence needs a bit of a boost. This will help because when you behave in a confident fashion, you appear more confident, those around you respond positively to this confidence and that, in turn, reinforces your self-confidence.

Inaction breeds doubt and fear. Action breeds confidence and courage. If you want to conquer fear, do not sit home and think about it. Go out and get busy. *Dale Carnegie*

Practise...
Standing tall.
Relaxing your shoulders.
Registering your contact with the earth and feeling grounded.
Breathing easily and comfortably.

Practise...
In your daily interactions with people you don't know – at the bus stop, with shop assistants and receptionists – take any opportunity to engage and talk, however briefly, acknowledging them and sharing a comment or smile. It's a good exercise, especially if you are, by nature, a little shy.

Practise...
Keeping a notebook. At the end of each day, write down three things that you have successfully achieved, done or enjoyed – however small – and about which you feel pleased and grateful. The following morning, re-read what you wrote and start each day from a place of confidence.

Practise...
Stepping outside your comfort zone. Embrace new opportunities. If you never challenge yourself, it's hard to build confidence. Recognise what you're good at, but take it a step further and build on it. Do one thing every day that challenges you: take a walk, sign up for that class, say hello to someone, read that book. Small steps taken regularly add up to increased confidence.

True life is lived when tiny changes occur. *Leo Tolstoy*

Practise...
Asking for help. We can't know everything – no one can – but one of the secrets of confident people is that they know *when* to ask for help, because

they know that we learn more when guided by someone who has the expertise we seek. It is not a sign of weakness to ask for help, but strength.

Practise...
Breaking down what you need to do into small chunks. Each step accomplished makes you feel more confident about the next. Building on this approach keeps you focused on the here and now and stops you getting anxious and stressed and feeling undermined about what comes next.

The secret of getting ahead is getting started. The secret of getting started is breaking your complex tasks into small manageable tasks, and then starting on the first one.

MARK TWAIN

Acting confidently – or 'fake it 'til you make it'

This may sound like a direct contradiction to being your own, best *authentic* self, but occasionally faking it is just another tool you can use when circumstances demand that you up your game.

> **Act the way you want to be and soon you'll be the way you act.** *Leonard Cohen*

Channel your inner confidence

This is where you focus on an occasion when you felt good about yourself, did something you were pleased with and felt confident: remember *that* feeling and use it now. Channel it into your current mindset with the words: ' *Yes, I can.*'

If you're presenting yourself with confidence, you can pull off pretty much anything.

KATY PERRY

WHEN DOES FAKING IT WORK BEST?

I would not recommend it for astronauts, lawyers, heart surgeons, rugby players, nuclear reactor engineers, or special-forces soldiers. It works great, however, if your goal is to change a personal trait, like your own self-confidence, courage, or self-efficacy. In other words, it doesn't work if you need specialised knowledge, skill, or training. It works very well for generalised traits that involve emotional resilience, courage, or motivation.

FRANKLIN VEAUX, AUTHOR OF *THE GAME CHANGER*

Your self-worth is determined by you. You don't have to depend on someone telling you who you are.

BEYONCÉ

Power walk

This is about physical confidence and the body language it expresses. Even when you're not feeling your most confident you can fake it by acting it: square up, take a breath and – as your grandmother would say – put your best foot forward. As you power walk, you connect with the ground in a positive way, and that reinforces your physical confidence. You know that song, the one that always makes you feel upbeat and strong? Aretha Franklin singing 'Respect'? Pharrell Williams singing 'Happy'? Handel's 'Hallelujah Chorus'? Whatever works for you, hear it in your head as you walk.

First impressions – why they count

You may not think it should matter, but it does: people make a first judgement about another person within three seconds of seeing them. That's right, *three seconds* – effectively, at first glance. That's not to say that an initial opinion can't be revised. It's also true that some people bring greater assumptions – even prejudice – to the table than others. The bottom line, however, is that first impressions count whether it's a first date, a job interview, or making a presentation to a roomful of strangers.

> **You never get a second chance to make a first impression.**
> *Andrew Grant*

To make this work in your favour and increase your self-confidence at the same time, forget the idea that first impressions don't matter, because they do. As someone once said, you can change the rules plenty once you get there, but first you've got to get there. Understand this, and you're halfway there.

Dress shabbily and they remember the dress; dress impeccably and they remember the woman.

COCO CHANEL

What you wear

When considering what to wear to make a positive first impression, remember that whatever you choose must be appropriate to the situation. Obviously, for a job interview you want to convey that you're serious about it while also reflecting the culture of the workplace you're applying to: a City job requires much more formal clothing than, say, working in a children's nursery where a sombre suit would look out of place.

Bear in mind that neutral blues and greys and more sombre colours like black and brown can convey seriousness, while brighter, bolder colours like red, orange or green can suggest greater creativity. Whatever you wear, it should be clean, pressed and not overtly sexy to make a good first impression. You will feel more comfortable and confident in clothes that fit you well, suit you, convey an accurate sense of who you are but are also appropriate to the situation.

Physical confidence

This can be learnt (see pages 49–55) and now is the time to demonstrate it in your posture. A straight back with relaxed shoulders may not come naturally, but it conveys confidence. And when you sit, sit up straight at the front of the chair, with both feet on the floor (which will help ground you), looking the other person in the eye. Avoid crossing your legs, jiggling in your chair or generally fidgeting.

> **Men acquire a particular quality by constantly acting a certain way.** *Aristotle*

Personal grooming

To convey confidence, and self-confidence, you need to look as if you take care of yourself. Make sure your hair is clean and tidy. For men, this extends to facial hair as well. Nails should always be clean and unbitten; a manicure isn't essential, and in some cases brightly coloured nail varnish might be inappropriate. Personal grooming should also extend to feet if they are going to be on show. Teeth should be clean and unstained, and your breath fresh. Any make-up should enhance rather than distract from your appearance and, again, should be event-appropriate.

Attitude

Given you have three seconds to make that first impression, how can you ensure you come across positively? Along with all of the above, this includes your attitude, how you carry and present yourself. Even if you are not feeling 100 per cent confident at that moment of first meeting, making sure you look someone in the eye, smile at them and greet them by name suggests confidence and gets you through that initial first stage. It may be that you make, or need to respond to, physical contact either by shaking hands or exchanging a hug. A positive attitude to this will show warmth of character, which inspires confidence, too.

Act as if what you do makes a difference. It does.

WILLIAM JAMES

Shaking hands

Shaking hands is a social convention that creates a space in which you look each other in the eye and make physical contact when you meet. It's an acknowledgement, an immediate social exchange and something that can usefully be employed to demonstrate equity between two people, too – which is why it's very useful for promoting confidence and indicating a confident attitude. For women in the workplace, in particular, it can be useful as a tactic that promotes self-assurance and equality.

- Always stand to shake hands. Be the first to extend your hand.
- Look the other person in the eye and smile.
- Make contact, palm to palm.
- Clasp firmly and shake once.
- Speak in greeting as you shake hands, using the other person's name.

Smile

This isn't always easy when you are feeling unconfident but the trick is to think something nice about the person you're interacting with. This helps a smile to be less forced, to be more genuine and to extend to the eyes. Smiling suggests warmth and engagement and promotes a sense of confidence in yourself that extends to others.

Addressing anxiety, taking risks & embracing the unknown

For many people, a common challenge to their confidence is feeling anxious. While some anxiety is a normal, predictable part of life and often a reasonable, short-lived response, sometimes it can feel overwhelming. If you are someone who feels that anxiety undermines your confidence, it can be useful to identify your personal triggers and devise a strategy to manage them.

Fear defeats more people than any other one thing in the world.

RALPH WALDO EMERSON

Breathe

When we're anxious, we tend to breathe shallowly and can even hyperventilate. Because this mimics how our bodies react in a fight or flight response, it automatically makes us *feel* more anxious. In this case our bodies are telling our minds we're anxious. In extreme situations, this hyperventilation can accelerate and even lead to a panic attack. So if we can utilise a way of breathing calmly, our bodies can tell our minds we're calm. This is when the breathing exercise (see page 53) can be a really useful tool for confidence. The trick is to practise it regularly so that it becomes a familiar tool, there when you need it.

GROUND YOURSELF

This is helpful if you start to feel overwhelmed by anxious thoughts. Look around and find:

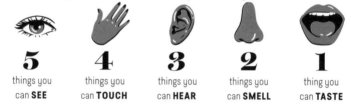

5	**4**	**3**	**2**	**1**
things you can **SEE**	things you can **TOUCH**	things you can **HEAR**	things you can **SMELL**	thing you can **TASTE**

Meditation

Many people find a meditative practice really useful in managing anxiety, both generalised anxiety and occasional extremes of it. However, for this to work, it needs to be learnt and practised regularly so it can be accessed at will. It's well worth exploring, even just as an adjunct to daily exercise.

Meditation is a little drop of perfume that suffuses the day with its grace. *R. D. Laing*

FIVE-MINUTE RELAXATION TECHNIQUE

This needs to be practised regularly so that you're familiar with it and can then access it whenever you need it.

- Sit comfortably.
- Close your eyes.
- Consciously relax your focus, taking it inwards.
- Work your way through muscle groups, consciously tensing then relaxing them – so you can feel the difference – focus particularly on the muscles of your upper back, shoulders, neck and face.
- Consciously calm the breath. Slowly breathe in for a count of five; hold for a count of three; release the breath evenly for a count of five. Repeat 10 times.
- Let any thoughts that come to mind drift pass without engaging with them.
- Suspend judgement of yourself, recent events, things to come.
- Return to the present with positive thoughts.

Get active

When we are anxious, we tend to generate more stress hormones, such as cortisol and adrenalin, which in turn makes us feel jittery and more anxious: a vicious circle. But one of the quickest ways of alleviating this is to move or exercise. Take a walk, jog, swim, do yoga; anything that focuses your nervous energy and uses it physically will help dissipate the stress hormones.

Don't ruminate

Going over and over the negative of whatever is making you anxious will reinforce it. Instead, use positive affirmation and statements that remind you that no feelings are final; you have evidence that you can do whatever it is you want to do, with confidence. Talk things through with a trusted friend and get some positive feedback, instead of ruminating or obsessing. Good social support is important for all of us and is one of the many ways we can feel more confident about life.

Worry never robs tomorrow of its sorrow, it only saps today of its joy.

LEO BUSCAGLIA

Look after yourself

Getting overtired, drinking too much alcohol or caffeine, missing meals, drinking too little water – all of these things can make us feel jittery and kick-start our stress hormones to compensate. These physical feelings imitate feelings of anxiety and can create a vicious circle. Either way, to function confidently, you need to feel on top of your game physically, too (see pages 49–55).

Let it go

Easier said than done, for sure, but sometimes just acknowledging anxiety for what it is – a passing phase – can be a helpful approach. Some people find that this tactic alone can reassert their confidence.

Nothing in the affairs of men is worthy of great anxiety.
Plato

Social confidence & dealing with nerves

If the idea of social occasions makes you nervous and you would like to feel more confident, it's good to know that there are some things you can do to make it easier to deal with your nervousness.

Are you shy?

Shyness comes from feeling awkward or apprehensive about new situations or meeting new people. This is different from being an introvert (see page 18), where spending time alone can be more energising than spending time in company, but while social events aren't always enjoyed, they're not feared. Most shy people want to connect but feel very self-conscious about their attempts to do so. A couple of ways around this are to arrange to go to an event with a friend or colleague, which can ease the initial anxiety on arrival; or to arrive on time, in order to avoid a bigger crowd that might intimidate you. Do what suits you best and makes you feel more confident.

What's the occasion?

Some social occasions can make us feel less confident than others; we are all different. Some of us might actually find smaller, more intimate occasions more difficult than larger, less personal ones. Or, the reverse. Either way, whatever the issue might be for you, there are things you can do to make it easier. First off, when you get an invitation – a relative's wedding, a colleague's birthday drinks, a first date – think it through and, perhaps, have a chat about it with a trusted friend. Get a handle on what it is that might undermine your immediate confidence; the dress code, for example. Not sure what to wear? Check it out beforehand. Nervous about giving a speech? Prepare and practise (see pages 125–131).

Life is like a camera... Focus on what's important. Capture the good times. Develop from the negatives. And if things don't work out... Take another shot! *Anon*

Breathing

Those breathing exercises (see page 53) you learnt for an occasion just like this? Now's the time to use the calm, steady breathing technique to help ground and focus you, taking your mind off any nerves.

Visualisation

Visualising the event you are going to attend can be helpful, if the thought of it makes you nervous. Creating a picture in your head of how you will confidently arrive, walk in, greet your host, accept a drink – the initial scenario – while also enjoying the anticipation of the event, can give you confidence. It's a bit like an actor rehearsing a part, or 'faking it' a little (see page 73).

> **Once we believe in ourselves, we can risk curiosity, wonder, spontaneous delight, or any experience that reveals the human spirit.** *e.e. cummings*

Listening

Listening well (see page 102) is an important part of social interaction – and something that can be a challenge if we are distracted by nerves. So, make a conscious effort to register someone's name, for example, and maybe use it the first time you talk to them to reinforce your memory of it. This will also help the other person relax, too, which can only be a good thing.

Show interest

People generally respond well when someone shows an interest in what they have to say and this can help your own confidence. If you are, by nature, a little shy or introverted, you may find that by facilitating a conversation in this way you deflect attention from yourself, which can be useful initially. Also, showing interest usually prompts the other person to do the same. Ask questions, but listen to the answers and move the conversation forward in response to these, give your own views, contribute personal anecdotes: in this way, good conversations are had.

The benefit of small talk

Many people deride small talk but on social occasions, especially with people you've just met, it can really help open up conversations. We usually start by exchanging names and then there are a number of straightforward options. For example, 'How do you know the host?' or, 'Did you have far to travel?' The answers might lead to other questions and an initial exchange of information on which you can build. You can also use something a little more personal. Try admiring a piece of clothing or jewellery, for example. At this first stage, don't make it too personal or about a physical feature – unless, perhaps, they are showing off a particularly flamboyant tattoo that commands attention!

Remember...

If all else fails, use the five-minute relaxation technique (see page 91). The truth is, very few of us are totally socially confident all of the time but what we can all do is find a way to manage our nerves. Taking the trouble to make someone else feel welcome and relaxed works both ways: it enables you to feel more confident, while being generous to them. It is also the essence of good manners to be thinking about other people and extending those same courtesies to them that we'd like extended to ourselves. Doing this, rather than focusing exclusively on ourselves and how we are feeling, can often open up communication and help us feel more confident about our own ability to function well socially.

You wouldn't worry so much about what others think of you if you realised how seldom they do.

ATTRIBUTED TO ELEANOR ROOSEVELT

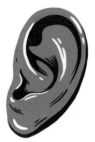

Importance of listening

What's listening got to do with confidence? Being an active listener – and there's a difference between *hearing* and *listening* – reaps its own rewards when it comes to promoting self-confidence.

Listening to someone is different from hearing something. Listening is a conscious process of engaging with the speaker with the intention of understanding what's being said and communicating with them. Active listening demonstrates the confidence of the listener and is a skill that can be learnt. It shows that the listener knows and understands the value that active listening brings to their relationships. It doesn't matter whether this skill is used with your boss, employees, children, friends or partner; used effectively, it will enhance your relationships, making you feel more confident about them.

> **Most of the successful people I've known are the ones who do more listening than talking.** *Bernard Baruch*

The word 'LISTEN' contains the same letters as the word 'SILENT'.

ALFRED BRENDEL

ACTIVE LISTENING

When we are actively listening, we give the speaker non-verbal clues that we are doing so in a variety of ways that create more confident communication. These non-verbal signs of active listening include:

- **Posture**: posture is open, friendly and relaxed, whether sitting or standing. The head tends to be inclined towards the speaker.
- **Eye contact**: this goes hand in hand with posture but make sure it's not too intense, because that could be intimidating or perceived as confrontational. Gauge what feels appropriate to the situation, and make eye contact natural, not unblinking or staring.
- **Smiling**: a gentle smile, as appropriate, can help soften eye contact and the facial expression, showing friendly attention to what is being said. It also encourages the speaker to continue speaking.
- **Mirroring**: this signals engagement, and the mirroring of facial expressions often comes into play when reflecting sympathy.
- **Not fidgeting**: and not looking at a watch, yawning, picking at fingernails or doodling; all of which signal lack of interest and attention.

However, remember that when you are feeling unconfident or nervous, it's easy to be distracted. This is when active listening can be particularly helpful. Also, it pays to focus well enough to remember, for example, someone's name when you're introduced for the first time (see page 98). This is why shaking hands on first meeting, marking that moment through touch and eye contact, and using a name in greeting, can be helpful for focusing attention.

Most people do not listen with the intent to understand; they listen with the intent to reply. *Stephen R. Covey*

In some emotional or intense circumstances, an active listener can use their skills to create an opportunity for the other person to speak freely and confidently – for example, in a therapeutic setting. This may not require full eye contact, but the other non-verbal cues remain the same. In addition, short, open-ended questions, affirmative nods and occasional words of assent can all encourage a reluctant speaker.

Courage is what it takes to stand up and speak; courage is also what it takes to sit down and listen.

SIR WINSTON CHURCHILL

Why did Winston Churchill say this? Because he understood that when you listen properly, even though you may not always like what you hear, it can be highly instructive. If you fail to hear something critical but which is to your advantage, then it's a missed opportunity. It takes confidence to know that you can utilise information from others, taking from it what is useful, because other people's experience and expertise can often teach us valuable lessons.

Dating

When it comes to our most personal, intimate relationships, dating is the process that gets us there: it's the trial and error of finding someone with whom to share time and possibly a future life together. And, for many, it's a challenge to their personal confidence.

Be the type of person you want to meet. *Anon*

Do I believe in computer dating? Only if the computers really love each other.

GROUCHO MARX

Dating in the twenty-first century is quite a different game to what it was even 20 years ago. In the past, the most common way people met was through their school, college or workplace, their social circle or families. Today, largely thanks to the internet, apps and social media, the circle in which you might meet is far, far wider. In fact, today it's pretty infinite and global. Which brings its own challenges. Expectations about how we meet may have changed, but the hopes that dating embodies remain the same: finding a partner with shared values, interests, ambitions and dreams, whatever our age, gender, race, colour or creed. A good relationship can be the source of our greatest self-confidence and, conversely, our greatest heartbreak.

How can you date with confidence?

First off, see dating for what it is. It should be relaxed and fun and a way to get to know someone – you make the rules here, remember. It's an opportunity to see if you are destined to be friends, or more than friends – or not. It's an opportunity to check out the other person, get to know them and see what might work for you both. If you like each other enough to go on a first date, let go of expectations and leave that list at home: just look for shared interests and see if the conversation flows. Bring your best self to the date, but don't feel you have to put on a show or try too hard; you're not auditioning for a lifelong position, it's just a date.

- Confident people don't define themselves by their relationships.
- Confident people set good boundaries and expect respect and courtesy from their partner, and behave in the same way.
- Confident people don't change themselves to fit the relationship; they look for a relationship that fits them.
- Confident people realise that if a relationship falls apart, it's not because they did something wrong.
- Confident people trust their instincts and their decisions.

Be kind

Given how easy it is to meet virtual strangers these days, it can be just as easy to dismiss them, or be dismissed in turn, without much thought. Being polite, respectful and kind, however you feel about your date, is just decent behaviour and no less than anyone can expect. So, have the confidence to behave well, however anyone else behaves – it costs nothing.

Be safe

One of the first rules of modern dating, whatever your age, is to date safely, especially when meeting someone for the first time. This is even more relevant today, as your date could be, essentially, a stranger. Whatever they've told you before you meet, you have no real idea if it's true. Bear that in mind and meet somewhere you'll feel comfortable, staying cautious about your personal information for the time being.

What I find powerful is a person with the confidence to be her own self.

OPRAH WINFREY

Work & business confidence

Building confidence at work is a process. It starts with getting a job, which is evidence of someone else having confidence in *you*: they believe you can do the job. That confidence builds through work experience, and through the proactive steps you take to achieve it.

Counter self-doubt

Self-doubt can affect our confidence if we think we can't do a job. It's often irrational, based on some imagined, perfect idea of how we ought to be, without recognising that we wouldn't have been given the job in the first place if we hadn't met our employer's criteria for it. Self-doubt is linked to imposter syndrome (see page 41) – the sense that we might get 'found out' in some way, which can be very undermining. Counter such self-doubt by focusing on the evidence of what you do well, gain confidence from that and then identify what areas might benefit from improvement.

Successful people have fear, successful people have doubts, and successful people have worries. They just don't let these feelings stop them.

T. HARV EKER

Continual professional development

This should be both a personal ideal and something that a company or organisation aspires to on behalf of its staff. Most work requires skills – some you bring with you and are transferable, while others can be fostered and learnt on the job. If you stretch yourself, seek new challenges and learn new skills, you'll stay motivated and your confidence will remain strong. Whether it's specific training for a job or team-building, for example, it should be a two-way street in terms of the commitment you bring to a job and the commitment your employer offers you. In this way, you can be confident about your continuing professional development and your employer can be confident that you are fully equipped to meet their expectations, too.

ARE YOU READY FOR THE NEXT WORK CHALLENGE?

- List your skills and accomplishments.
- List your experience and expertise.
- See how far they apply to a job you already have, a promotion you'd like or another job you want to apply for.
- Assess what other skills or training you might need and work out whether you can do this at your current workplace or as an extra-curricular activity.
- Consider any changes you might want to make and how these could be realised.
- Seek help, advice and support from someone you admire to support your aims.
- Whatever your ultimate goal, identify the steps that lead towards it and address each one in turn.

Fellow workers

Few of us can work in glorious isolation – it's not much fun anyway – and often our employment is dependent on being able to work as part of a team in one way or another. Teams are often put together to balance complementary skills and personalities and need to be managed by good team leaders. Sometimes clashes occur and managing differences between yourself and co-workers is also a learnt skill. Some people manage it better than others, but becoming confident in our interpersonal skills takes time and experience, and this needs to be borne in mind. Some workplaces fit together better than others, but it's always important to find solutions if problems arise. Good managers want confident employees, not least because they work better, so take any problems you can't solve yourself to your immediate manager.

My confidence is easy to shake. I am well aware of all of my flaws. I am aware of all the insecurities that I have.

TAYLOR SWIFT

Don't over-personalise

A workplace is a workplace and there are various expectations; one is that you will confidently do the job you were hired to do. Along the way, you may need some feedback or constructive criticism to help you do this. This may be done formally at an appraisal or informally via a chat, but should be seen for what it is – something that is helpful to you and that can be built on and utilised to your advantage. You can seek feedback, or ask for help, at any point if you are struggling with something. This is a mark of confidence: confidence in the fact that you will get the help you need and will then be able to work more effectively.

Feedback

When asking for feedback, try to make it specific rather than asking, 'How am I doing?', which can have the unwanted effect of making you sound or look insecure, and could be counter-productive. Better to ask how the way you approach a task could be more effective, or better realised, or delivered more efficiently. That opens up opportunities for your manager to tell you about the things you're doing well, which is a confidence-booster, while helping him or her to depersonalise what could be improved. Most people want to be positive and helpful and this approach makes it easier, while also creating confident relationships at work.

Choose your battles

Occasionally the workplace can yield tension and confrontation. It may be a personality clash or it may be a conflict of ideas. Bear in mind your place in the scheme of things and evaluate what the advantages and disadvantages might be to you of choosing a particular battle. You will be more successful, and become more confident as a result, if you choose battles that align most closely with your own values, feelings and behaviour, as the outcome is more likely to be in your favour.

Confident leadership

Leaders are partly born, partly made. Some people seem to be more instinctively able to lead than others; they actively like it and they do it well. However, it takes a degree of skill and experience to become a really confident leader. Training and mentoring often feature in the development of leaders, which builds their confidence so that leadership skills are developed, enhanced and improved.

A good leader inspires people to have confidence in the leader; a great leader inspires people to have confidence in themselves. *Eleanor Roosevelt*

Job interviews

Whether you are applying for a part-time job while you're at college or returning to work after a major career break, the same rules apply – although the stakes may be a little higher in the latter situation!

Choose a job you love, and you will never have to work a day in your life. *Confucius*

EASY AS A, B, C & D

Prior to the interview, your application will be the first point at which a decision is made about your suitability for the job. If you are submitting a CV or online written application, make sure that you:

A Read the job specification carefully.

B Answer all sections accurately and as completely as possible.

C Make your personal statement relevant to the job for which you're applying.

D Make sure all spelling and punctuation is correct.

Preparation

Once you have applied and been invited to an interview, preparation is crucial. Do some background research on the company or organisation. So much information is now available online, and there is often a company or organisation website, so make sure you have taken a look – especially at its structure, history, clients and corporate presentation. The more familiar you are with the company and the job for which you are applying, the more confident you will feel about your interview.

You may, as is common in some industries, have been asked by the HR department to prepare something quite specific to deliver as part of the interview: a presentation perhaps, or some ideas to be discussed. If you are given a brief for this, make sure you understand it. And remember – it is a sign of confidence to ask for clarification if you're not sure about anything.

You may also have the opportunity for an informal chat beforehand. If this is offered to you, think about how it might be useful to your preparation – and take up the offer.

> **One important key to success is self-confidence. An important key to self-confidence is preparation.** *Arthur Ashe*

The three key components of a job interview are:

> *Can you do the job?*

This goes beyond actual qualifications and is where you have to demonstrate that your skills and experience are aligned to the job's specific requirements. Whatever you have put on your application you are likely to be asked about, so make sure you can provide brief examples that show actual and relevant evidence that you can do the job in question.

> *Do you want the job?*

Interviews work both ways: it's as much an opportunity for you to see if you want the job as to whether they want to give it to you.

> *Will you fit in?*

One of the points of the interview for the employer is to meet someone who, very often, has to fit into a team, replacing someone else or bringing something new and beneficial to an existing team. This makes it quite personal but can also explain why the 'fit' doesn't always work. This works both ways, too: does the company or organisation have the same values, attitude and approach as your own? Will you be happy to fit in with them?

On the day

> First impressions count (see pages 79–84). An immediate assessment will be made about you the minute you walk through the door – so make sure you use this to your advantage.

> Whatever you do, don't be late. Check the route to the interview venue carefully and consider the most efficient way to ensure you're on time. Aim to arrive a little early, so you have time to collect your thoughts.

> Dress appropriately. Some industries and jobs are very formal, others less so. Either way, aim to be smart and well presented, and avoid wearing clothes or make-up that could be overtly distracting from the role you are interviewing for. Keep things a little understated, unless you work in a highly creative industry where you know flamboyance is the norm!

> Feeling a little nervous is to be expected, but don't let your nerves overwhelm you (see page 91).

Whenever you're asked if you can do a job, tell 'em 'Certainly I can!' Then get busy and find out how to do it.

THEODORE ROOSEVELT

After the event

If you got the job – congratulations! But if you didn't, it's perfectly reasonable to ask for feedback that might be useful to you for future applications or interviews so you can see this as a good learning experience. Feedback can actually help your confidence by knowing where you did well and in what areas you might need to improve. In most cases, asking for feedback after a job rejection is accepted industry practice. A quick checklist for this can help you structure the feedback process:

> * **Keep it brief** – this is not a chat with a friend, but a formal process.
> * **Keep it formal** – the decision has been made, so remember this is not an opportunity to make excuses or give explanations but to gain valuable feedback.
> * **Don't make it personal** – however difficult such rejections can be, it isn't personal so don't make it so. Keep to the essentials that will serve you in the future: what you did well and what you could do better.
> * **Show your appreciation** – it's not easy for someone to explain why they needed to reject you so be sure to thank them for their feedback.

Presentation skills & public speaking

Public speaking is the number one fear, according to some pundits, but don't let this put you off! There's so much you can do to improve and polish your presentation skills – using a lot of the tools covered earlier in this book – and if you put in the work, it's something in which you really can gain in confidence.

Your voice

When you speak in public, you need to be heard. You may need to use a microphone; with smaller groups, you may just need to be able to project your voice enough to ensure that they can 'hear you at the back'!

Generally, for public speaking you need to speak:

› A little lower – this is especially true for women.
› A little more slowly.
› More loudly than usual – but not shouting!

This will immediately help you speak more clearly. As long as you do speak clearly, an accent of any sort can be engaging and work in your favour.

You also need to breathe properly (see page 53) when you speak aloud. Breathe from the abdomen rather than from the upper chest, as this will help with projection and with steadying your nerves. Pausing can be used to good effect, too, to allow your audience time to grasp an idea, for dramatic effect and – also! – to allow you to breathe properly.

The most precious things in speech are the pauses.
Ralph Richardson, actor

Practise

It's also worth practising what you want to say out loud, because the first time you speak in this way – with or without a microphone – can feel very different, and you want to be comfortable with your voice at that moment. Practising speaking aloud, either by reading out loud or reciting a poem, will also allow you to get used to your voice. This will help you overcome any slight wobble in your voice that nerves can sometimes cause.

REMEMBER THAT LESS IS MORE

No one ever complained that a speech or presentation was too short. And practising can help you with timing. Only through rehearsal will you see how long it takes. So, whether you've been given a 15-minute slot, or one hour, which includes a 20-minute question-and-answer session, rehearse and you will know beforehand that you can deliver to your brief.

Body confidence

Feeling grounded really helps here, especially when you're nervous. Remember that poise and body confidence (see pages 49–55) also take practice. These tools are important because we usually have to present or speak standing up. If your legs feel wobbly it will undermine your confidence and how you use your body language to deliver. Faking it and looking relaxed (even if you don't feel it at first) will help your confidence, too.

Prepare

This goes without saying. You need to know what the aim of your presentation or speech is, what point or points you want to make or need to get across. Once you have identified this, build your presentation around it. Keep it as simple and as straightforward as you can. Understand the purpose of what you're doing – whether this is participating in a school debate, giving a work presentation, or making a speech at a wedding – the context of what you're doing will help you with the content. It needs to be appropriate to the occasion.

If you can't write your message in a sentence, you can't say it in an hour. *Dianna Booher*

Actual preparation might entail writing out what you want to say and gathering everything together in an order that's relevant to how you want to say it. Don't just read it aloud; you need to present it to your audience. It has to be delivered – 'performed', if you like – in such a way as to engage your listeners. Very few people can do this completely off the cuff unless they are very experienced. Preparation and practice will give you the confidence you need.

It usually takes me more than three weeks to prepare a good impromptu speech.

MARK TWAIN

PowerPoint presentations

A note on PowerPoint: like any visual aid, this should enhance your presentation, not provide you with a crutch. It needs to work for you, not distract your audience – either through boredom or irrelevance – from what you're trying to say.

Aaron Weyenberg, who has worked on multiple slide presentations for the world-famous series of TED Talks, says, 'Frequently in good presentations, photos serve well in a metaphorical or conceptual sense, or to set a backdrop tone for what the audience is hearing from the presenter, and not necessarily to communicate actual content.'

WEYENBERG'S TOP TIPS

- Think about your slides last.
- Create a consistent look and feel.
- Avoid slides with lots of text.
- Use simple photos that enhance meaning.
- Use storytelling.
- Have a focused message that you want your audience to retain.

Ask for help – and feedback

If you know someone who you feel can give you some pointers and feedback that will help your confidence, then ask. Rehearse. Ask them to watch you and tell you what works and what might need improving. It's quite hard to evaluate how well you're preparing without feedback, so if there's an opportunity for you to do this, it can really help.

And finally...

Arrive in ample time prior to the event. Scoping the venue will give you greater confidence when it comes to actually making your speech or giving your presentation. This is especially important if you need to use a microphone or other media aids. Even if it's just plugging your laptop into their system, you need to know it will work – and also, what provision you can make if it doesn't!

A few mistakes do not a fiasco make. Professionals throw them off casually but file them away to reinvent as an endearing anecdote in later presentations. Make them part of the performance! Put them behind you and keep going whatever happens. *Ruth Bonetti*, Speak Out, Don't Freak Out

Confident you!

Given all the opportunities today for education, travel, socialising and global connectivity, in many ways we've never had it so good and our self-confidence should be at an all-time high.

There is, however, something of a downside, particularly for today's young people. While online connectivity has grown spectacularly over the last 20 years, the opportunities for real-time connectivity seem to have diminished. More and more young people communicate online, rather than in person. Safe indoors, they are losing out on opportunities to interact person to person, stretch themselves physically or solve problems alone, making them more risk-averse and less confident about their ability to function outside their immediate, secure environment. Social media means that while every move they make is documented or relayed via Facebook, Instagram, text or online messenger – it's not in person. And this is important: we cannot be confident of our personal interaction and relationships, our ability to manage risk and solve problems, unless exposed to them.

IN 2015, IN THE UK, A STUDY PRODUCED BY THE SKY ACADEMY IN COLLABORATION WITH YOUGOV, FOUND THE FOLLOWING:

33%

One in three young people surveyed are 'not confident'.

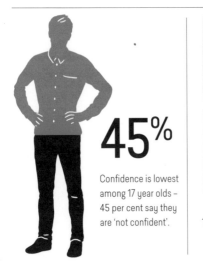

45%

Confidence is lowest among 17 year olds – 45 per cent say they are 'not confident'.

37%

Nearly two in five social-media users aged 14–17 surveyed online feel they can be more confident on social media than in person.

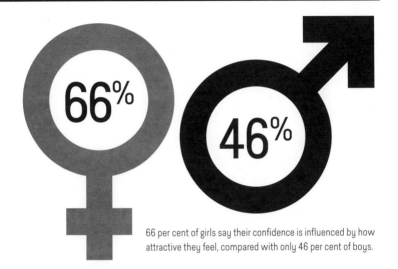

66 per cent of girls say their confidence is influenced by how attractive they feel, compared with only 46 per cent of boys.

97 per cent of parents and 90 per cent of young people consider confidence as an important factor for achieving success, as opposed to being naturally clever (72 per cent of parents; 67 per cent of kids).

The good news, however, is that with the right attitude, tools and support, everyone can improve their self-confidence.

Nothing is more powerful than confidence. In my career it was my parents who first gave me the encouragement and confidence to overcome boundaries and achieve my goals. It was then about hard work and determination to build the skills I needed to succeed.

JESSICA ENNIS-HILL, OLYMPIC GOLD MEDAL WINNER

Acknowledgements

In the writing of this book, I'd like to thank all my friends for their insights and wisdom along the way – they know who they are!

I'd also like to thank my publisher, in particular Kate Pollard, Kajal Mistry and Hannah Roberts, for their continued support. Thanks are also due to Julia Murray, whose talent for illustration and design ensures my words are brought to life.

Once again, I thank my sons, Josh and Robbie, for being a continued part of my daily life and for all that they've taught me.

Appendix

Further reading

Presence, Amy Cuddy
(Orion Publishers, 2016)

Silent Messages, Professor Albert Mehrabian
(Wadsworth Publishing Company, 1972)

Self-Compassion, Kristin Neff, PhD
(Yellow Kite, 2011)

About the author

Harriet Griffey is a journalist, writer and author of numerous books focused on health. Along with *I want to be confident*, she is the author of four other books in this series: *I want to sleep, I want to be calm, I want to be organised* and *I want to be happy*, all published by Hardie Grant. Other published books include *The Art of Concentration* (Rodale, 2010), *How to Get Pregnant* (Bloomsbury Publishing, 2010), and *Give Your Child a Better Start* (with Professor Mike Howe; Penguin Books, 1995). She originally trained as a nurse and writes and broadcasts regularly on health and health-related issues, and is also an accredited coach with Youth at Risk (www.youthatrisk.org.uk).

Harriet

Index

A

acting confidently 73–7
active listening 101–5
adolescence 21
  statistics 134–5
anxiety 21, 42, 87–93
appearance 45–7, 80–3
  job interviews 122
appraisals 116–17
assertiveness 46
attitude 83
authenticity 35–7
avoidance strategy 29

B

barriers to confidence 29–32, 39–42
  addressing 29–30
Beckett, Samuel 9
being yourself 35–7
Beyoncé 76
body confidence 49–55, 82
  personal space 60–1
  power walking 76
  and public speaking 128
body language 46–7, 55, 57–61, 82
  active listening 101–5
  power walking 76
breathing 52–3, 97
  and anxiety 90
  and public speaking 126
Brown, René 66

building confidence 32
Buscaglia, Leo 92

C

Cain, Susan 20
catastrophising 42
challenges at work 114–15
Chanel, Coco 81
Churchill, Sir Winston 104–5
clothing 45, 80–2
  job interviews 122
cognitive behavioural therapy (CBT) 21, 30
colleagues 116
comfort zone, stepping outside of 70
communication 57–61 see also body language
  non-verbal 59
  online 133
comparison with others 25
confidence
  barriers to 29–32, 39–42
  building 32
  definition 7–8
  quiz 13–15
  statistics 134–5
conflicts at work 116, 117
continual professional development 114–15
core strength 50
courage 104

D

dating 107–11
Davenport, Barrie 10
doubts 113
dress 45, 80–2
  job interviews 122

E

Emerson, Ralph Waldo 88
Ennis-Hill, Jessica 136

esteem 25
exercise 50
  and anxiety 91
  benefits of 55
extroverts 18, 36
eye contact 46, 47, 57, 102, 104
eye rolling 58

F

facial expression 57
failure 8
'fake it 'till you make it' 73–7
fear 88 see also anxiety
feedback
  job interviews 123
  presentations 131
  workplace 116–17
fight or flight response 90
first impressions 79–85

G

Gandhi, Mahatma 64
Gates, Bill 18
gestures 59
grounding yourself 55, 90

H

hands
  gestures 59
  shaking others' 84, 104
help, asking for 70–1
hyperventilating 90

I

imposter syndrome 41–2, 113
inner confidence, channeling 73
inner critic 30, 39–41
inner voice 63–7, 73
interviews 119–23
intimate distance 60
introverts 18, 20, 36, 95
  and shyness 21

J

James, William 83
job applications 120
job interviews 119–23

L

leadership 117
Lee, Bruce 30, 37
listening skills 46, 98, 101–5

M

Marx, Groucho 104
meditation 90–1
Mehrabian, Albert 57
muscle tone 49, 50
music 76

N

narcissism 25
Neff, Kristin 26
negative thoughts 30, 91
nerves see anxiety; social confidence
Nin, Anaïs 40

O

online communication 133
online dating 108–11
overthinking 42

P

panic attacks 90
Perry, Katy 74
personal distance 61
personal grooming 82–3
personal space 60–1
personality 17–20
physical confidence 49–55, 82
    power walking 76
    and public speaking 128
positive affirmations 41, 63–7, 73, 91
posture 49, 50, 55, 58–9, 70, 82
power walking 76

PowerPoint 130–1
practising confidence 69–71
presentations 125–31
    job interviews 120
    PowerPoint 130–1
    preparation for 128
public speaking 125–31
    preparation for 128

Q

quiz 13–15

R

relaxation techniques 90–1
Roosevelt, Eleanor 99
Roosevelt, Theodore 123
ruminating 91

S

self-acceptance 36
self-assurance 24
self-belief 24
self-care 92
self-compassion 26
self-confidence 8–10
self-criticism 26, 39–41
self-doubt 113
self-esteem 25
self-indulgence 26
self-sabotage 41
self-worth 23
shaking hands with others 84, 104
shyness 21, 95
small talk 98–9
smiling 84
social confidence 17–18, 95–9
social distance 61
social media 133
    and dating 108–11
    statistics 134
speeches 125–31
    preparation 128

strangers
    dating 110
    talking to 29–30, 70, 98–9
Streisand, Barbara 18
stress 91, 92 see also anxiety

T

t'ai chi 55
teamwork 116
thoughts
    negative 30, 91
    positive 41, 63–7, 73, 91
touching 59
Twain, Mark 71, 130

V

visualisation 98
voice
    public speaking 125–6
    tone of 58

W

Weyenberg, Aaron 130–1
Winfrey, Oprah 110
women
    public speaking 126
    in the workplace 84
workplace 113–17
    continual professional
    development 114–15
    feedback & appraisal 116–17
    fellow workers 116
    leadership 117
worry 92, 99 see also anxiety;
negative thoughts

Y

yoga 55

I want to be confident by Harriet Griffey

First published in 2017 by Hardie Grant Books

Hardie Grant Books (UK)
52–54 Southwark Street
London SE1 1UN
hardiegrant.co.uk

Hardie Grant Books (Australia)
Ground Floor, Building 1
658 Church Street
Melbourne, VIC 3121
hardiegrant.com.au

British Library Cataloguing-in-Publication Data. A catalogue record
for this book is available from the British Library.

ISBN: 978-1-78488-081-1

Publisher: Kate Pollard
Senior Editor: Kajal Mistry
Editorial Assistant: Hannah Roberts
Internal and Cover Design: Julia Murray
Internal and Cover Illustrations: Julia Murray
Copy Editor: Charlotte Coleman-Smith
Proofreader: Clare Hubbard
Indexer: Cathy Heath
Colour Reproduction by p2d

Printed and bound in China by 1010

10 9 8 7 6 5 4 3 2 1